THE CANTICLES

THE CANTICLES

A faithful and inclusive rendering

from the Hebrew and the Greek into

contemporary English poetry, intended primarily for

communal song and recitation. This translation is

offered for study and for comment by the International

Commission on English in the Liturgy.

LTP

LITURGY TRAINING PUBLICATIONS

ACKNOWLEDGMENTS

The International Commission on English in the Liturgy (ICEL) acknowledges with gratitude the editorial committee and the subcommittee and its consultants who have ably and generously assisted at various stages of this project. It should be noted that some of the subcommittee members served for as many as 14 years. ICEL also thanks those parishes, religious communities, liturgical commissions and individuals who sent comments as the work progressed.

EDITORIAL COMMITTEE

Lawrence Boadt, CSP
Mary Collins, OSB
John Dzieglewicz, SJ
Peter Finn
Joseph Wimmer, OSA

SUBCOMMITTEE MEMBERS AND CONSULTANTS

Peter Barry
Lawrence Boadt, CSP
Rita Burns
Daniel Coughlin
Mary Collins, OSB
Margaret Daly
John Dzieglewicz, SJ
Peter Finn
Leslie Hoppe, OFM
Roderick MacKenzie, SJ
Mary McGann, RSCJ
John McGuckin
Marjorie Moffatt, SNJM

Joseph Mulrooney
Irene Nowell, OSB
James Schellman
Eileen Schuller, OSU
Geoffrey Boulton Smith
Pamela Stotter
Carroll Stuhlmueller, CP
Michael Suarez, SJ
Francis Sullivan, SJ
Thomas Troeger
Elizabeth-Anne Vanek
Christopher Willcock, SJ
Joseph Wimmer, OSA

IMPRIMATUR

In accord with canon 825, §1 of the Code of Canon Law, the National Conference of Catholic Bishops hereby approves for publication the *Liturgical Psalter,* a translation of the Psalms submitted by the International Commission on English in the Liturgy.

> William Cardinal Keeler, D.D., J.C.D.
> President, National Conference of Catholic Bishops
> Washington, D.C., January 5, 1995

Editor: Gabe Huck. Art: Linda Ekstrom. Design: Kerry Perlmutter and Anna Manhart. Canticle introductory lines: Elizabeth-Ann Vanek. Afterword: Staff of the International Commission on English in the Liturgy

Library of Congress Cataloging-in-Publication Data
    Catholic Church.
       [Liturgy of the hours (U.S., et al.)]
       The Canticles: a faithful and inclusive rendering from the Hebrew and the Greek into contemporary English poetry, intended primarily for communal song and recitation.
       Companion volume to The Psalter.
       "This translation is offered for study and for comment by the International Commission of English in the Liturgy" — T.p.
       1. Catholic Church — Liturgy — Texts.   I. International Committee on English in the Liturgy.   II. Title.
    BX2000.A4   1996   96-19567
264' .024 — dc20   CIP

ISBN 1-56854-152-X (hardcover)   HCANT
ISBN 1-56854-160-0 (paperback)   PCANT

CONTENTS

xi

FOREWORD
Gabe Huck

The books of the Hebrew Bible and of the Christian New Testament do not keep the boundary between what we identify as prose and what we identify as poetry. In scripture, we are in the presence of wonderful ways of using language that resist our zeal to classify. So we stand in a long procession of scripture readers who have readily found long or short passages in the scripture that call out for use in our own prayer. The psalter is set apart in the Bible as an entire prayer book of such useful and formative texts, but psalm-like lines — sometimes a few, sometimes many — have been taken by Jews and Christians from the narrative books, the wisdom literature, the prophetic texts. And Christians have found their own earliest poetry and song embedded in the letters and other books of the New Testament.

Scripture texts that, like the psalms, have been readily used as ritual prayers have been called "canticles" or songs by some in the Christian tradition. In an essay, which follows the texts of the canticles, Irene Nowell discusses the content, form and spirit of these scripture canticles.

There are far more canticles in the scriptures than are presented in this volume. This is a sampler of scripture's songs or poems. It includes all the canticles that are presently found in the Liturgy of the Hours of the Roman Catholic tradition. That is, all of these texts are prayed as part of morning or evening prayer or at the office of readings. Some of these canticles will also be found in the lectionaries for Mass or other rites. The order in which these canticles are presented is based on the arrangement of the biblical books that is generally used by Roman Catholics and many others.

This is a companion volume to *The Psalter*. The work of this translation was done by the same scholars working under the auspices of the International Commission on English in the Liturgy (see the acknowledgment pages). The same principles of translation were used for these canticles; these principles are explained in the Afterword to this volume.

As in *The Psalter,* each canticle is prefaced by a brief summary line prepared for this edition. The divisions of the canticles into stanzas and the groupings of the stanzas are the work of those who prepared the translation.

This book is offered as the labor of scholars and artists to fashion canticles for assemblies to sing and individuals to recite. Those who have prepared these texts have struggled for fidelity to the Hebrew and Greek texts and for the words and cadences of contemporary poetry. Their work intends to be in continuity with the English translations we have known until now, but it is clearly something new. Speak it, listen to it. If it has strength, if it has validity, that will emerge only with familiarity. Only when one begins to know some of these texts by heart will they be tested and proved. That is the nature of such speech. The intention of the International Commission on English in the Liturgy is that this translation be evaluated and revised before the end of the 1990s. The comments of all who use this translation are welcome and should be directed to the publisher at the address found on the acknowledgment pages.

Bound to *The Psalter,* may these canticles open our lips as individuals and as communities, day by day and through the seasons of our lives.

EXODUS

CHAPTER 15:1—18

THE CANTICLE OF MOSES AND MIRIAM

WHEN GOD'S RIGHT ARM IS RAISED IN POWER,
EARTH AND SEA SWALLOW THE ENEMY.
GOD'S PEOPLE CROSS OVER IN SAFETY
TO THE PLACE OF PROMISE.

---

1   I sing of the Lord,
    great and triumphant:
    horse and rider
    are cast into the sea!

2   The Lord is my strength,
    the Lord who saves me —
    this is the God I praise,
    the God of my ancestor.

3   True to the name "Lord,"
    our God leads in battle,
4   hurls Pharaoh's chariots
    and army into the sea.

    The best of their warriors
    sink beneath the Reed Sea,
5   sink like rocks to the bottom,
    lie covered by the deep.

6   Your right arm, Lord,
    is majesty and power,
    your raised right arm
    shatters the enemy.

---

7 Awesome your power:
you hurl down enemies,
you blaze forth in anger
to consume them like stubble.

8 One blast from your nostrils
and the waters pile high,
the waves pull back
to stand firm as a wall.

9 The enemy thinks, "Pursue them,
seize them and all they have,
feast on all their wealth,
draw the sword and destroy them."

10 But you send another blast;
the sea swallows them,
like lead they sink
in the terrifying waters.

11 Who can rival you, Lord,
among the gods?
Who can rival you,
terrifying in holiness?

Awesome this story,
fearful your wonders:
12 you stretched out your hand,
the earth swallowed them.

13 By your love you guide
this people you redeemed,
your power clears their path
to your holy place.

14 When nations hear, they shudder:
the Philistines writhe in fear,
15 all the princes of Edom
tremble in their terror,

all the chiefs of Moab
shake beyond control,
all the people of Canaan
16 melt away in dread.

Your mighty arm strikes terror,
they fall silent as stone,
while your people, Lord, cross over,
your own people cross over.

17 You brought and planted them, Lord,
on the mountain you chose,
where you make your dwelling,
the temple you built by hand.

18 The Lord rules for ever and ever! □

DEUTERONOMY

CHAPTER 32:1–12

THE CANTICLE OF MOSES

**IN ANCIENT TIMES, GOD ENFOLDED ISRAEL IN LOVE,
GUIDING, PROTECTING, LIKE A VIGILANT EAGLE
HOVERING OVER ITS LITTLE ONES.
TODAY, FOREVER, GOD ALONE IS GOD.**

---

1 Hear me, heaven and earth,
   listen to what I say.
2 May my thoughts fall like rain,
   may my words cling like dew,
   like gentle rain upon tender grass,
   like showers upon seedlings.
3 I will praise the Lord's name,
   I will tell of God's greatness.

◆

4 God is the rock,
   whose works are perfect,
   whose ways are right,
   a God faithful and true,
   just and without deceit.

5 But the corrupt and headstrong
   treat God with contempt,
   they are no longer God's children.

6   Is this how you thank God,
    you slow-witted fools?
    Did God not father you,
    create you, and provide for you?

◆

7   Remember ancient times,
    think back to ages past.
    Ask your parents; they will tell you,
    your elders will teach you.

8   When God gave the nations their land,
    dividing the human race,
    the Most High set boundaries for peoples,
    equal to the number of gods.

9   The Lord adopted Jacob,
    claimed Israel as a people,
10 finding them in the wilderness,
    in the wild and howling wasteland,
    enfolding them with care,
    keeping a loving eye on them.

11 Like an eagle rousing its young,
    hovering over its little ones,
    spreading its wings to carry them,
    to bear them up in flight,
12 the Lord alone guided Israel;
    there is no other God.   □

1 SAMUEL

CHAPTER 2:1−10

THE CANTICLE OF HANNAH

GOD REVERSES HUMAN EXPECTATIONS,
LIFTING UP THE POOR, CASTING DOWN THE WEALTHY,
BREAKING THE POWER OF THE WICKED.
GOD WALKS WITH THE FAITHFUL.

---

1 I acclaim the Lord's greatness,
source of my strength.
I devour my foe,
I say to God with joy:
"You saved my life.

2 Only you are holy, Lord;
there is none but you,
no other rock like you."

3 God knows when deeds match words,
so make no arrogant claims.

4 The weapons of the strong are broken,
the defenseless gain strength.

5 The overfed now toil to eat,
while the hungry have their fill.

The childless bear many children,
but the fertile learn they are sterile.

6 The Lord commands death and life,
consigns to Sheol or raises up.

7 God deals out poverty and wealth,
   casts down and lifts up,
8 raising the poor from squalor,
   the needy from the trash heap,
   to sit with the high and mighty,
   taking their places of honor.

   God owns the universe
   and sets the earth within it.
9 God walks with the faithful
   but silences the wicked in darkness;
   their power does not prevail.

10 God's enemies will be broken,
   heaven thunders against them.
   The Lord will judge the earth,
   and give power to the king,
   victory to the anointed.   □

1 CHRONICLES

CHAPTER 29:10−13

THE CANTICLE OF DAVID

**PRAISE TO THE GOD OF ISRAEL, THE GOD OF CREATION.
TO THE SOURCE OF ALL GLORY AND BLESSINGS, PRAISE!**

---

10   Blest are you for ever, Lord,
      God of our father Israel.
      Power, splendor, greatness,
      glory and honor are yours.

11   The whole universe is yours.
      You are peerless in majesty,
12   from you flow wealth and glory.

      You command all:
      your hand is strength,
      your hand makes strong.

13   And so we thank you, God,
      we praise your splendid name.   ☐

TOBIT

**TURN, TURN TO THE LIVING GOD.
PRAISE THE GOD OF HEALING AND COMFORT.
THEN, IN DELIGHT, GOD WILL TURN TOWARD YOU.**

---

1 Blest be the living God,
   reigning for ever,
2 who strikes, then heals,
   casts deep into the grave,
   and raises up from utter ruin;
   no one eludes God's hand.

3 Praise God, Israel,
   among the nations
   where you are scattered.

4 Announce God's greatness
   wherever you are.
   Extol the Lord to everyone:
   the Lord is our God,
   who fathered us,
   God for ever.

5 Once God punished you,
   because you did wrong.
   Now God comforts all of you
   and gathers you from the nations
   where you have been scattered.

---

6 When you turn your heart and mind
to live rightly before God,
then God will turn to you
and never hide again.

Match your praise
to all God has done for you.
Bless the Lord of justice,
who rules for ever.

Though captive, I praise the Lord.
I tell a sinful nation
how strong and great God is.

Sinners, turn back,
act justly before God,
who may yet respond
with pardon and delight.

7 As for me, I extol the Lord,
my heart rejoices in God Most High. ☐

TOBIT

CHAPTER 13:8–11, 13–15

O JERUSALEM, HERE GOD WELCOMES THE EXILE.
HOLY CITY, MAY THERE BE DANCING IN YOUR STREETS.

8 Give witness to God's glory,
in Jerusalem give praise!

9 Jerusalem, holy city,
God punished you,
because your citizens did wrong.
Yet God will spare
the children of the just.

10 Make your praise worthy of God
who rules the ages,
that you may be a joyful city
where the temple rises again,
where God welcomes every exile
and loves for ever all who suffer.

11 A light shining over all the earth
will draw to your holy name
distant nations and peoples.
They will bring gifts
for the ruler of heaven.

All generations
will offer sacrifice here.
They will name you,
"Chosen Forever!"
13 Go now and celebrate
with the children of the just,
gathered to praise the living God.

14 Jerusalem, holy city,
blest are they who love you
and delight in your peace,
blest who mourn when you suffer.
They shall dance in your streets,
brimming over with joy.

15 Bless the Lord who reigns for ever. ☐

JUDITH

AT GOD'S WORD, AT GOD'S BREATH, ALL CREATION CAME TO BE.
IN GOD'S PRESENCE, IN GOD'S GLORY,
THE COSMOS BENDS.

2 Shake tambourines! Clash cymbals!
Strike up a song to my God!
Sound a new music of praise!
3a Praise and call on God's name!

13 I sing my God a fresh new song:
"Grandeur and glory are yours, Lord,
with power that astonishes all;
no rival can match your might.

14 "Let all creation bend to you:
for you spoke, and they took shape;
you breathed, they came alive.
No one can resist your voice.

15 "Mountain peak and ocean depth
quake to their inmost core.
Rocks melt like wax when you appear,
while you spare those who stand in awe." ☐

PROVERBS

**WISDOM SPREADS HER FEAST:
FAT FOODS AND SPICED WINES UPON HER TABLE.
COME EAT! COME DRINK! LONG LIFE!**

---

1 Wisdom has built her house
    and carved its seven pillars.
2 She has butchered the meat,
    spiced the wine, and set her table.
3 She has dispatched her servant women.

    She calls from the town heights,
4 "Let the simple-hearted come."
    She tells the unschooled:
5 "Come, taste my bread,
    drink my spiced wine.
6 Give up your ignorance and live,
    walk the straight path of insight."

10 Wisdom begins when God is revered;
    knowledge of the Holy One is insight.

11 "I will add days,
    even years to your life."
12 Wisdom wins you friends,
    boasting cuts you off.   □

WISDOM

IN THE FIRE-TRIAL, THE JUST TRIUMPH.
REFINED LIKE PUREST GOLD, THEY LIVE WITH GOD.

---

1 The hand of God
keeps the souls of the just
free from torment.
2 In the eyes of a fool
they are no more,
their death a disaster,
3 their departure the end of them.
But they are at peace.

4 In our mortal view,
they were punished,
but they gained what they hoped for:
never ending life.

5 What they faced is nothing
compared to their blessing:
God tested them
and found them worthy.
6 Pure as fired gold,
they were to God
a fruitful sacrifice.

7 On judgment day
 they will flare up like sparks
 that ignite the stubble.
8 They will judge nations
 and govern peoples
 while the Lord rules for ever.

9 Whoever trusts God
 will grasp this truth.
 Whoever is faithful
 will live with God in love.
 Grace and mercy
 belong to the chosen.
 God watches over the holy. □

WISDOM

**WISDOM SITS BY YOUR THRONE, O GOD.
MAY SHE BE OUR COMPANION, OUR GUIDE TO HOLINESS.**

---

1 Merciful God of my ancestors,
  with a word you created all things;
2 in wisdom you made humankind
  to care for your creatures
3 with holiness and justice,
  to rule with upright heart.

4 Give me Wisdom who sits by your throne;
  never forget I am your child,
5 your servant born of your handmaid,
  frail, given little time,
  with limited grasp of your laws.
6 Yet even someone perfect
  is nothing without the Wisdom
  that comes from you.

9 With you is Wisdom;
  she knows your works,
  was there when you made the world.
  She sees what you judge as best,
  knows what is right in your commands.

10 Send her from heaven,
     from your glorious throne
     to be my companion,
     to teach me your will.

11 Her understanding is complete;
     she guides me wisely
     through all I must do,
     and guards me with her clear light.   □

WISDOM

WONDERS UPON THE WAY — COOLING SHADE, FLAMING STARS,
SAFE PASSAGE AND TRIUMPHANT SONG.
PRAISE THE WONDERS OF WISDOM.

---

17 Wisdom paid the holy ones
    wages for their labor.
    Wonders marked the way she led them.
    She was shade by day,
    a flame of stars at night.

18 She brought them through the Reed Sea,
    walked them through great waters.
19 She drowned their enemies
    in the churning waves
    and cast them to the shore.

20 Then the just despoiled
    the corpses of the godless
    and sang to you, Lord,
    praising with one voice
    your power and holy name.

21 Wisdom gave words
    to lips that were mute
    and ready speech to infants.   □

WISDOM

CHAPTERS 16:20—21, 26; 17:1A

**BREAD OF SWEETNESS, FOOD FOR ANGELS, HEAVENLY MEAL —
THIS IS GOD'S WORD, PLEASING TO EVERY TASTE.**

---

20 You hand-fed your people
with food for angels,
heaven's bread:
ready to eat,
richly satisfying,
pleasing to every taste.

21 Eating this bread,
they tasted your sweetness,
the perfect meal
for their deepest hunger and hope.

26 The children you love
will learn this, Lord:
it is your word,
not the bounty of fruits,
that feeds and preserves
your faithful ones.

17:1a Great are your judgments,
beyond calculation! □

SIRACH

CHAPTERS 14:20; 15:3−5A, 6B

**WISDOM'S FEAST REFRESHES;
GIVES INSIGHT, UNDERSTANDING, KNOWLEDGE.**

---

20 Happy those who feast on Wisdom
and savor her knowledge.
15:3 She will nourish and refresh them:
her bread is insight,
her drink is understanding.

4 They will lean on her and not stumble,
trust her and not be disgraced.
5a She will raise them above their peers,
6b that their name may always endure. □

SIRACH

CHAPTER 31:8–11

RICHES BEYOND WEALTH, RICHES OF INTEGRITY,
RICHES CHOSEN ABOVE SELF-GAIN, FOR THE BENEFIT OF ALL.

---

8 Happy are the rich
who still have their integrity,
who are not corrupted by money.

9 Name them,
that we may esteem them;
they have acted
for the benefit of everyone.

10 Let them take pride
in passing the test:
they had their chance
to do wrong but did not;
they had their chance
to choose evil but would not.

11 No wonder their wealth is secure
and the assembly sings their praise. □

SIRACH

CHAPTER 36:1–7, 13, 16–22

THEN WILL THE WORLD SEE GOD'S GLORY,
THEN WILL THE WORLD KNOW WHAT WE KNOW:
THAT GOD ALONE IS GOD.

---

1 Show us mercy, God of all,
2 teach every land to fear you.
3 Strike boldly against the enemy,
 display your power.

4 Make them an example of your glory,
 as we once showed them your holiness.
5 Then they will know what we know:
 there is no God but you.
6 Forge new signs, new wonders
7 with your strong right hand.

13 Gather every tribe of Jacob
16 to reclaim its birthright.
17 Be kind to Israel, your firstborn,
 to the people who bear your name.

18 Deal gently with Jerusalem,
 your holy city,
 where your throne is fixed.
19 Fill Zion with your splendor,
 your temple with your glory.

20 Make real the vision
prophets spoke in your name;
keep faith with what you began.
21 Reward those who hope in you,
prove the prophets right.

22 Answer the pleas of the faithful
and favor us as always.
Then the world will know
that you are God for ever. □

SIRACH

CHAPTER 39:13–16A

**LIKE THE SWEET FRAGRANCE OF ROSES,
LET OUR PRAISE RISE TO YOU, O GOD.**

---

13 Hear me, devoted children,
and bloom like roses
beside the stream.
14 Be fragrant as incense,
rich as the lily in bloom.

Spread your perfume abroad
by singing hymns
and praising the Lord
for doing great things.

15 Glorify and proclaim God's name
with song and music
on lyre and harp.
Give thanks and shout with joy,
16a "All God does is good!" □

ISAIAH

CHAPTER 2:2–5

ALL YOU NATIONS, ALL YOU SEEKERS OF PEACE,
LEAVE BEHIND YOUR WEAPONS.
CLIMB, CLIMB THE LORD'S MOUNTAIN AND ENTER GOD'S HOUSE.

2 In the final days
the temple summit will tower
above the highest hills and mountains.
All nations will stream toward it.

3 Strangers will come and say:
"Let us climb the Lord's mountain
to the house of Jacob's God,
who will teach us the way of truth
and the path we should walk."
From Zion comes instruction,
from Jerusalem, God's word.

4 God will end conflict between nations,
and settle disputes between peoples;
they will hammer swords to plows,
and spears to pruning knives.

5 Nations will not take up arms,
will no longer train for war.
House of Jacob, come,
let us walk in the light of the Lord.   □

ISAIAH

CHAPTER 9:1–6

**GREAT LIGHT IN DARKNESS! GREAT JOY!
A CHILD IS BORN AND THERE SHALL BE PEACE.
HALLELUJAH!**

---

1 The people who walk in darkness
   see a great light;
   on a land shadowed by death
   light now shines.

2 What joy you bring them! What gladness!
   They celebrate before you
   like workers after harvest,
   like soldiers claiming the spoils.

3 As on the day at Midian
   you break their captor's prod,
   the bar on their backs,
   the heavy yoke.

4 Every soldier's boot,
   every blood-soaked uniform
   will be burned as fuel for fire.

5 For a son is born, a gift to us,
   robed with power, honored with titles:
   Wise Counselor, Divine Hero,
   Father Forever, Prince of Peace.

6 As he rules from David's throne,
his power expands
till there is lasting peace
with fairness and justice in every age.

This shall come about,
for the mighty Lord wills it.   ☐

ISAIAH

CHAPTER 12:1–6

DRINK DEEPLY FROM GOD'S SAVING WELL.
LET THE WATERS OF CONSOLATION
GIVE YOU STRENGTH, TRUST AND JOY.

---

1 I praise you, Lord!
   When your rage turned on me,
   you turned it away
   and now you console me.

2 God is my savior,
   my trust knows no fear;
   God's strength is my strength,
   yes, God is my savior.

3 With joy you will draw water
   from God's saving well;
4 then you will say to each other,
   "Praise the Lord! proclaim God's name!"

   Tell the world what God does,
   make known this majestic name.
5 Sing the wonders God works,
   recount them in every land.

6 Shout and sing for joy,
   citizens of Zion,
   for great among you
   is the Holy One of Israel!   □

ISAIAH

CHAPTER 26:1–4, 7–9, 12

FIX YOUR HEART ON GOD,
YEARNING, LONGING, TRUSTING, SEEKING.
HONOR TO GOD'S NAME!

1 Our city is strong,
  its ramparts and walls
  are God's saving work.
2 Throw open the gates
  to a just nation,
  one that keeps faith.

3 You guard the faithful in peace,
  they fix their hearts on you.
4 Trust in the Lord always,
  our enduring rock.

7 For the just you make the road
  level, smooth, and straight.
8 We walk the road you cut,
  looking for you, O Lord.
  We seek to honor your name.

9 I long for you by night,
  my whole being yearns for you.
  For by your judgments
  the world learns justice.
12 Our peace is your gift, Lord,
  our good deeds your work. □

ISAIAH

CHAPTER 33:2–10

ARISE, O LORD, WITH JUSTICE, WITH MERCY.
SCATTER THE VIOLENT, BRING HEALING TO THE EARTH.
NOW, LORD!

---

2 Show mercy, Lord,
we look to you.
Be our strength at dawn,
our savior in crisis.

3 When you roar,
people flee.
When you rise,
nations scatter.

4 We gather spoil
like locusts,
rushing upon it
in a swarm.

◆

5 God is exalted —
at home in the heights,
yet filling Zion
with judgment and justice.

6 Your fortune depends on these.
  They are a treasure of wisdom,
  knowledge, awe, and saving power.

◆

7 Look! Heroes weep openly,
  messengers of peace cry bitterly.

8 Highways lie desolate,
  travel comes to a standstill.
  People break contracts,
  disregard witnesses,
  care about no one.

9 Earth languishes and mourns,
  Lebanon is disgraced, decayed,
  Sharon a desert,
  Bashan and Carmel stripped bare.

◆

10 The Lord says:
   "Now I will rise.
   Now I will raise myself.
   Now I will surely rise!"   □

ISAIAH

CHAPTER 33:13−16

13 Listen, my people,
far-off and nearby.
See what I do,
know my power.

14 Terror grips the wicked in Zion;
the godless shake with fear.
Who can face the fiery judgment?
Who can endure the lasting flames?

15 Only the honest in word and deed
who refuse to exploit others,
who turn down bribes,
who will not hear of bloodshed
or dare to imagine crimes.

16 They live secure and safe
as in a mountain fort
with plenty to eat and drink.   □

ISAIAH

CHAPTER 38:10−14, 17−20

DEATH HAD ME IN ITS GRIP,
TEARING BONES, UNRAVELLING LIFE,
BUT GOD SNATCHED ME FROM THE PIT.
I WILL SING TO THE GOD WHO SAVES!

---

10 In the prime of my life
     I felt death reaching for me,
     calling me to Sheol's gates,
     cutting short my days.

11 I was stunned to think
     I will never again see God,
     never again see a human face
     here on this earth.

12 My life collapsed
     like a tent pulled down,
     like cloth cut from a loom
     before it is finished.
     Day and night I face death.

13 God like a lion
     tears my bones apart.
     I groan until dawn.
     Day and night I face death.

14 Shrill as a crane,
   mournful as a dove,
   I weep before heaven,
   "My world is collapsing;
   Lord, hold me up."

17 You brought good from my pain.
   You cast aside my sins
   and from the deadly pit
   snatched me away.

18 Who thanks you in the grave?
   Death does not praise you.
   The dead in Sheol
   no longer hope in you.

19 Only those alive,
   alive like me,
   can thank you
   and tell their children
   how faithful you are.

20 The Lord saved me.
   Let us make music
   and sing in the temple
   as long as we live.   □

ISAIAH

CHAPTER 40:10−17

GOD ALONE HOLDS THE POWER,
SCOOPING UP OCEANS AND NATIONS,
WEIGHING MOUNTAINS AND HILLS,
YET GATHERING THE FLOCK, TENDERLY.

10 Look! the Lord comes.
    What power God holds!
    See what spoils the victor brings!

11 As the shepherd tends the flock,
    the Lord gathers the lambs
    in a warm embrace
    and leads the nursing sheep.

12 Who can scoop up the oceans
    or span the heavens with one hand?
    Who can hold the earth in a measure,
    weigh the mountains on scales,
    the hills on a balance?

13 Who directed the Lord's spirit?
    What mortal counseled God?
14 Whose advice did God seek?
    Whose teaching on the way of justice?
    Whose guidance on the path to wisdom?

15 The nations are like a drop of water,
   a speck of dust on the scales.
   The Lord lifts up islands like sand.

16 Lebanon has neither wood enough
   nor beasts enough for sacrifice.
17 In God's sight the nations are nothing.
   They are empty as a void.   □

ISAIAH

CHAPTER 42:10−16

WITH THE FURY OF A WARRIOR,
WITH THE BIRTH CRIES OF A WOMAN IN LABOR,
GOD SPEAKS FOR THE LOST AND THE BLIND.

---

10 Sing the Lord a new song.
    Let the sea with its creatures,
    the coastland and its people
    fill the world with praise.

11 Let every village and town,
    from Kedar on the plain
    to Sela in the hills,
    take up the joyful song.
12 Sing glory to the Lord,
    give praise across the world.

13 The Lord strides like a hero
    who rouses fury
    with a great battle cry
    and charges against the enemy.

14 "I have kept quiet too long,
    too long held back.
    Like a woman in labor
    I now scream and cry out:

---

15 "I will lay waste mountains and hills
    and stunt all their greenery.
    I will dry up rivers and pools
    and create an arid wasteland.

16 "I will lead the blind safely
    along strange roads.
    I will make their darkness light,
    their winding ways straight.
    I will do all this,
    I will not fail them." ☐

ISAIAH

CHAPTER 45:15–25

GOD, OUR CREATOR, SPEAKS:
TURN TO ME ALONE FOR HELP AND DELIVERANCE.
COME TO ME, YOU EXILES, FOR I WILL BRING YOU HOME.

15 You are an unseen God,
O saving God of Israel.

16 Makers of idols will be shamed
and paraded in disgrace.

17 But you, Israel, will never be shamed,
for your God upholds you for ever.

18 Thus says the Lord,
creator of the heavens,
God who formed the earth
and fixed it firm,
not a place of chaos,
but good to live in:
"I am the Lord.
There is no other.

19 "I did not speak in secret
from some dark land.
I did not say to Israel,
'Seek me in chaos.'
I am the Lord.
I speak the truth,
I say what is just.

20 "Gather together, you exiles,
   come out from the nations
   who are foolish enough
   to parade their idols
   and bow to gods unable to save.

21 "Speak out, present your case.
   Consult among yourselves.
   Who foretold this in ancient times?
   Was it not I, the Lord?
   There is no other God but me,
   no God to help and deliver,
   no one but me.

22 "Turn to me for rescue,
   all you in foreign lands,
   for I am God.
   There is no other.

23 "On my word I swear:
   I speak only truth
   that shall not be revoked.
   To me every knee shall bend,
   every tongue shall swear:

24 "From God alone
   comes victory and strength.
   All who defy the Lord
   shall stand in disgrace.
25 In the Lord shall Israel
   triumph and glory." ☐

ISAIAH

CHAPTER 49:7–13

YOU DESPISED AND ENSLAVED,
I WILL MAKE A FEAST FOR YOU ON BARREN HEIGHTS
AND GIVE YOU DRINK FROM COOLING SPRINGS.

---

7 The Lord, the Holy One,
Israel's redeemer speaks
to a nation despised,
enslaved by tyrants:

"Kings will see and rise,
princes will bow in awe,
for the Lord, holy and true,
has favored Israel.

8 "I have heard and helped you
on the day of salvation.
I give you power to stand
as my witness before the nations.
I restore your land
and raise it from its ruin.

9 "I tell prisoners: You are free,
come out into the light.
You will feast on your way,
find food on barren heights.

10 "No one will hunger or thirst,
or suffer the scorching sun,
for the Lord cares for them,
guides them to cooling springs.

11 "I will cut a mountain road,
build a level highway.
12 See, they travel from afar.
Look north, west, and south!

13 "Sing out, heaven and earth;
mountains, shout for joy:
the Lord embraces Israel,
comforts a suffering people." □

ISAIAH

CHAPTER 61:6–9

NO LONGER SHAMED, YOU WILL SERVE OUR GOD.
YOU AND YOUR CHILDREN
WILL DWELL SECURE IN THE LORD'S BLESSING.

6 All of you will be priests,
   servants of the Lord our God.
   You will enjoy the wealth of nations
   and feast on their plenty.

7 Because you were doubly shamed
   and disgrace was all you had,
   you will soon rejoice for ever,
   twice blest in your land.

8 I, the Lord, love justice,
   I hate stealing and fraud.
   True to myself, I reward you,
   give you a lasting covenant.

9 Your children will be known
   and stand out among the nations.
   All who see them will say
   they are blest by the Lord.   □

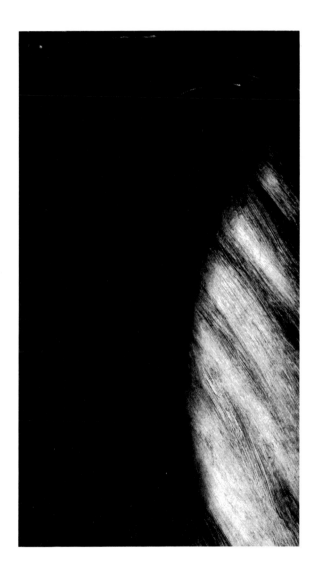

ISAIAH

CHAPTERS 61:10 — 62:7

THE LORD DELIGHTS IN YOU.
NO LONGER FORSAKEN OR BARREN,
YOU ARE THE BELOVED,
MARRIED TO YOUR GOD WHO HONORS YOU.

---

10 I sing out with joy to the Lord,
  all I am delights in God,
  for the Lord has dressed me
  in robes of justice and victory,
  like a groom wearing a garland
  or a bride arrayed in jewels.

11 As earth causes seed to sprout,
  and gardens make plants grow,
  so justice and praise spring from God
  for all the nations to see.

62:1 For Zion's sake I speak out,
  for Jerusalem I do not rest,
  till her victory shines like the sun,
  blazes out like a torch.

2 The world will see your deliverance,
  all kings witness your glory.
  They will know you by a new name
  which the Lord will give you.

3 Your walls and towers will shine forth,
  a royal crown in God's hand.

4 They will no longer call you Forsaken,
  nor your land Barren.
  Beloved will be your name,
  and your land will be called Married.
  For the Lord delights in you,
  and your fields will be fertile.

5 As a young man marries a wife,
  your Builder will marry you.
  As a groom delights in his bride,
  the Lord will honor you.

6 "On your walls, Jerusalem,
  I have posted guards
  to stay alert
  both day and night."

  Stay awake, you advocates,
7 and give God no rest
  till Jerusalem is built up
  to become earth's crown.   □

ISAIAH

CHAPTER 63:1–5

**IN RED-STAINED CLOTHES,
THE MIGHTY SAVIOR TREADS THE WINE PRESS,
TRAMPLES THE GRAPES AND WINS THE VICTORY.**

---

1 Who is this
marching from Edom,
coming from Bozrah
in red-stained clothes?

Who is this,
so splendidly dressed,
striding along with great power?

"I bring news of my victory,
I, the mighty savior."

2 Why are your clothes
splashed with red,
like those who crush grapes?

3 "I trod the winepress
alone, unaided.
In my fierce anger
I trampled them down.
Their juice splashed over me
and stained my clothes.

4 "My heart was set
   on a day of vengeance,
   to win back my own
   in my hour of triumph.

5 "I looked for help,
   but there was none,
   no one stood by me;
   my own arm brought victory,
   my anger kept me strong." □

ISAIAH

**BE GLAD FOR JERUSALEM
AND DRINK YOUR FILL,
FOR GOD NURSES YOU AND COMFORTS YOU,
HOLDING YOU CLOSE.**

---

10 Rejoice with Jerusalem!
 Be glad for her,
 all who love her.
 Share her great joy,
 all who know her sadness.

11 Now drink your fill
 from her comforting breast,
 enjoy her plentiful milk.

12 For this is what the Lord says:
 "Look! to her I extend
 peace like a river,
 the wealth of the nations
 like a stream in full flood.
 And you will drink!

 "I will carry you on my shoulders,
 cuddle you on my lap.
13 I will comfort you
 as a mother nurses her child.

 "Jerusalem will be your joy.
14a Your heart will rejoice to see it.
 You will flourish like grass in spring." ☐

JEREMIAH

**IT IS NOT THE TEMPLE
BUT RIGHT ACTION WHICH SAVES.**

---

2 Hear God's word, Judah,
all who enter these gates
to bow before the Lord.

3 The Lord of hosts,
the God of Israel says this:
"Reform your way of life
and I will dwell here with you.

4 "Put no trust in this lie:
The temple of the Lord!
The temple of the Lord!
The temple will save me!

5 "But if you truly correct
the way you live
and deal justly with each other,
6 not cheating the stranger,
the orphan or widow,
not spilling innocent blood
or letting false worship divert you,

7 "then I will dwell with you here
in the land I gave your people
long ago and for ever."   □

JEREMIAH

CHAPTER 14:17–21

**ZION IS CRUSHED, JUDAH REJECTED.
WE ACKNOWLEDGE OUR GUILT —
DO NOT ABANDON US, O GOD!**

---

17 Day and night
my tears never stop,
for my people are struck,
my daughter crushed
by a savage blow.

18 I see the dead slain in the fields
and people starving on city streets.
Priest and prophet wander about,
not knowing where to turn.

19 Lord, have you nothing
but contempt for Zion?
Have you completely rejected Judah?
Why have you inflicted wounds
that do not heal?

We long for peace,
we long for healing,
but there is only terror.
20 We have sinned against you
and we know it, God;
we share our people's guilt.

21 For the sake of your name,
    do not abandon us.
    For the honor of your throne,
    remember your covenant,
    do not break your oath.   □

JEREMIAH

CHAPTER 17:7–8

TRUST IN GOD ALONE.
EVEN IN THE DRY DAYS, YOU WILL BEAR FRUIT.

---

7 They are blest who trust in God,
who trust in the Lord alone.
They are like trees near a stream
stretching their roots to the water.

8 They fear no heat wave,
their leaves are always green.
When drought comes they have no worry,
they still produce their fruit. □

JEREMIAH

CHAPTER 31:10−14

**LAUGHTER AND DANCE,
RICH FOOD AND PLENTY!
GOD GATHERS THE SCATTERED FLOCK,
LEADING ISRAEL IN JOY.**

---

10 Nations! Hear God's word,
tell your distant shores,
"God gathers the scattered flock,
guides Israel like a shepherd."

11 The Lord has saved Jacob's people,
loosened the enemy's grip.
12 They reach Zion shouting for joy,
thrilled with the goodness of God:

they see grain and oil and wine,
new lambs and young calves;
they thrive like a watered garden
never to wither again.

13 Young girls break into dance,
the young and old join in,
for I turn their grief to laughter,
ease their sorrow with joy.

14 I serve my priests rich food,
I fill my people with plenty. □

LAMENTATIONS

CHAPTER 5:1–7, 15–17, 19–21

REMEMBER OUR SUFFERINGS, LORD.
SEE OUR DISGRACE.
PLUNDERED AND POOR, WE ARE WORN OUT WITH GRIEF.

---

1 Remember, Lord, what we suffer,
   look down and see our disgrace.
2 Outsiders plunder our wealth,
   foreigners live in our homes.

3 We are orphans without fathers,
   our mothers live as widows.
4 They make us pay for water,
   buy kindling for the fire.
5 They drive us under the yoke,
   wear us out, give us no rest.

6 We begged help from Egypt,
   we cried to Assyria for bread.
7 Our people died with their sins,
   but still we carry their guilt.

15 Our joy has turned to mourning,
    our dancing into grief.
16 The laurels fall from our heads;
    sad because we sinned,
17 our hearts grow sick
    and tears cloud our eyes.

19 But you, Lord, rule for ever,
   your throne outlasts the ages.
20 Why have you forgotten us,
   left us alone so long?

21 Bring us back to you, Lord;
   we will gladly come.
   Give us good days
   like those of old.   □

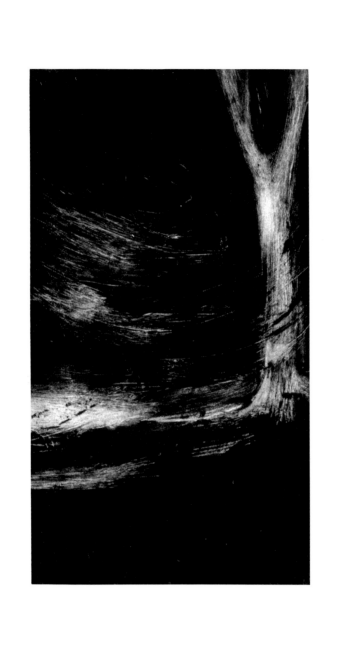

EZEKIEL

CHAPTER 36:24–28

GOD, YOU MAKE ALL THINGS NEW.
WASH US, CLEANSE US,
BREATHE YOUR SPIRIT INTO US.

---

24   I will draw you from the nations,
      gather you from exile
      and bring you home.

25   I will wash you in fresh water,
      rid you from the filth of idols
      and make you clean again.

26   I will make you a new heart,
      breathe new spirit into you.
      I will remove your heart of stone,
      give you back a heart of flesh.

27   I will give you my own spirit
      to lead you in my ways,
      faithful to what I command.

28   Then you will live in the land,
      the land I gave your ancestors.
      You will be my people
      and I will be your God.   □

DANIEL

CHAPTER 3:26–27, 29, 34–41

THE CANTICLE OF AZARIAH

CRUSHED IN HEART AND SPIRIT,
WE HAVE ONLY OUR TEARS TO OFFER YOU, O GOD.
WE STRAYED FROM YOU; DO NOT ABANDON US.

---

26 Blest are you, Lord,
  God of our ancestors,
  worthy of praise
  and renowned for ever.

27 Your works are true,
  your ways straight,
  your judgments sound,
  all your actions just.

29 We broke your law,
  we strayed from you,
  sinning in every way.

34 For the sake of your good name,
  do not abandon us,
  do not break your oath.
35 Think of your beloved Abraham,
  your servant Isaac, your holy Israel,
  and do not withhold your love.

36 You promised them descendants
countless as the stars,
like sand on the shore.
37 Yet we are the weakest of nations,
disgraced before all by our sins.

38 We have no king,
no prophet, no leader,
no burnt offering, no sacrifice,
no gift, no incense, no temple,
nowhere to find mercy.

39 Let a crushed heart and spirit
mean as much as countless offerings
of rams and sheep and bulls.
40 Let this be our sacrifice today,
let our loyalty win your favor,
for trust in you brings no shame.

41 Our hearts are completely yours.
We fear yet seek your presence.
Do not shame us.   □

DANIEL

CHAPTER 3:52–57

THE CANTICLE OF SHADRACH, MESHACH AND ABEDNEGO

**BLEST ARE YOU, GOD,
ALWAYS, EVERYWHERE, BY ALL CREATURES!**

---

52 Blest are you, God of our ancestors,
   praised and lifted above all for ever!
   Blest your holy name, full of wonder,
   praised and lifted above all for ever!

53 Blest are you in your temple of glory,
   acclaimed and honored for ever!
54 Blest are you who see the depths
   from the cherubim throne,
   praised and lifted above all for ever!

55 Blest are you enthroned in majesty,
   praised and lifted above all for ever!
56 Blest are you beyond the stars,
   acclaimed and honored for ever!

57 All you creatures, bless our God,
   acclaimed and exalted for ever!   □

DANIEL

CHAPTER 3:56–88

THE CANTICLE OF SHADRACH, MESHACH AND ABEDNEGO

STARS, GALAXIES, DRY LAND AND SEAS,
ANGELS AND CHILDREN OF EARTH, GIVE PRAISE!
NIGHT AND DAY, WINTER AND SPRING,
ALL GREEN THINGS, ALL CREEPING THINGS,
ALL CREATURES OF AIR, BLESS GOD FOREVER!

---

56 Bless God beyond the stars.
Give praise and glory.
57 Bless God, heaven and earth.
Give praise and glory for ever.

◆

58 Bless God, angels of God.
Give praise and glory.
59 Bless God, highest heavens.
Give praise and glory.

60 Bless God, waters above.
Give praise and glory.
61 Bless God, spirits of God.
Give praise and glory.

62 Bless God, sun and moon.
Give praise and glory.
63 Bless God, stars of heaven.
Give praise and glory for ever.

◆

64 Bless God, rainstorm and dew.
Give praise and glory.
65 Bless God, gales and winds.
Give praise and glory.

66 Bless God, fire and heat.
Give praise and glory.
67 Bless God, frost and cold.
Give praise and glory.

68 Bless God, dew and snow.
Give praise and glory.
69 Bless God, ice and cold.
Give praise and glory.

70 Bless God, frost and sleet.
Give praise and glory.
71 Bless God, night and day.
Give praise and glory.

72 Bless God, light and darkness.
Give praise and glory.
73 Bless God, lightning and clouds.
Give praise and glory for ever.

◆

74 Bless God, earth and sea.
Give praise and glory.
75 Bless God, mountains and hills.
Give praise and glory.

76 Bless God, trees and plants.
Give praise and glory.
77 Bless God, fountains and springs.
Give praise and glory.

78 Bless God, rivers and seas.
Give praise and glory.
79 Bless God, fishes and whales.
Give praise and glory.

80 Bless God, birds of the air.
Give praise and glory.
81 Bless God, beasts of the earth.
Give praise and glory for ever.

◆

82 Bless God, children of earth.
Give praise and glory.
83 Bless God, Israel.
Give praise and glory.

84 Bless God, priests of God.
Give praise and glory.
85 Bless God, servants of God.
Give praise and glory.

86 Bless God, just and faithful souls.
Give praise and glory.
87 Bless God, holy and humble hearts.
Give praise and glory.
88 Bless God, Hananiah, Azariah, and Mishael.
Give praise and glory for ever.

◆

56 Bless God beyond the stars.
Give praise and glory.
57 Bless God, heaven and earth.
Give praise and glory for ever. □

HOSEA

GOD DELIGHTS IN FAITHFUL LOVE,
IN HEARTS THAT SEEK TO KNOW THE LORD.

1 Let us return to the Lord
   who tore us apart
   but now will heal us;
   who struck us down
   yet binds our wounds;
2 who revives us after two days,
   raising us up on the third,
   to live in God's presence.

3 Let us seek to know the Lord,
   whose coming is sure as dawn,
   who descends like the rain,
   spring rain renewing the earth.

◆

4 What can I do with you, Ephraim?
   What can I do with you, Judah?
   Your love is but a morning mist,
   a dew that vanishes early.

5 So I cut them down by my prophets,
   slew them with my words;
   my judgment blazes like the sun.
6 For I take delight
   not in sacrifices,
   but in loyal love;
   not in holocausts,
   but in the knowledge of God.   □

HABAKKUK

CHAPTER 3:2–4, 13A, 15–19

NO MATTER THE FEAR, NO MATTER THE WOE,
YOU ARE OUR STRENGTH, OUR SAFETY.

---

2 They told me what you did, O Lord;
I listened, struck with awe.
Show your strength again,
act quickly for us,
not in anger but with compassion.

3 Now God comes from distant Teman,
the Holy One from Mount Paran.
God's brilliance fills the skies,
its grandeur lights the earth.
4 It blazes with a blinding flame
that conceals God's might.

13a You rise to save your people,
to rescue your anointed.
15 You ride your horses through the sea
and make the oceans rage.

16 I shake at their roar,
my stomach churns, my voice fails,
my knees buckle, I fall!
I wait for the day of agony
to overwhelm my foes.

17 Even if the fig tree fails
and vines bear no fruit,
if olives yield no oil
and fields no grain,
if sheep stray from their pens
and cattle from their stalls,
18 still I will glorify the Lord,
still rejoice in God my savior!

19 The Lord, my strength,
lets me run like a stag
and leap the highest mountain.   ☐

ZEPHANIAH

CHAPTER 3:8–13

IN RAGE AND CHAOS GOD WILL CLEANSE ISRAEL, SHELTERING THE FAITHFUL REMNANT.

---

8 The Lord says: "Expect me
to rise in witness against you,
for I shall gather the nations,
summon the kingdoms,
and pour out my rage against them.
The fire of my anger
will consume the whole world.

9 "But then I will change
the people's speech;
I will purify their lips
to speak God's name,
and unite their hearts
to serve the Lord.

10 "From beyond the rivers of Cush
my exiles will come to me,
faithful ones with gifts of grain.

11 "On that day I will lift the shame
of your sins against me,
I will wipe out your pride
and allow no arrogance among you.
You will not worship yourselves
on my holy mountain.

12 "I will leave among you
   a humble, lowly people
   who find their shelter
   in the Lord's name alone.

13 "This remnant of Israel
   will do no wrong,
   will speak no lies,
   will never deceive.
   They will rest and be fed
   where no one can hurt them." ☐

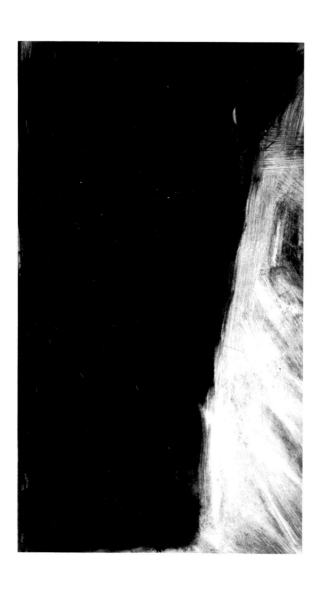

LUKE

CHAPTER 1:46–55

THE CANTICLE OF MARY

GOD'S GREATNESS IS MY DELIGHT,
GOD'S MERCY SHATTERS INJUSTICE.
REMEMBER GOD'S PROMISE!

---

46 I acclaim the greatness of the Lord,
47 I delight in God my savior,
48 who regarded my humble state.
Truly from this day on
all ages will call me blest.

49 For God, wonderful in power,
has used that strength for me.
Holy the name of the Lord!
50 whose mercy embraces the faithful,
one generation to the next.

51 The mighty arm of God
scatters the proud in their conceit,
52 pulls tyrants from their thrones,
and raises up the humble.
53 The Lord fills the starving
and lets the rich go hungry.

54 God rescues lowly Israel,
recalling the promise of mercy,
55 the promise made to our ancestors,
to Abraham's heirs for ever. □

LUKE

THE CANTICLE OF ZECHARIAH

**FROM THE GRIP OF HATRED, FROM THE CLUTCHES OF DEATH,
GOD PROMISES TO SAVE US,
TO LEAD US IN PATHS OF PEACE.**

---

68 Praise the Lord, the God of Israel,
who shepherds the people and sets them free.

69 God raises from David's house
a child with power to save.
70 Through the holy prophets
God promised in ages past
71 to save us from enemy hands,
from the grip of all who hate us.

72 The Lord favored our ancestors
recalling the sacred covenant,
73 the pledge to our ancestor Abraham,
74 to free us from our enemies,
75 so we might worship without fear
and be holy and just all our days.

76 And you, child, will be called
Prophet of the Most High,
for you will come to prepare
a pathway for the Lord
77 by teaching the people salvation
through forgiveness of their sin.

78 Out of God's deepest mercy
   a dawn will come from on high,
79 light for those shadowed by death,
   a guide for our feet on the way to peace.   □

LUKE

CHAPTER 2:29–32

THE CANTICLE OF SIMEON

**NOW GOD'S SERVANT HAS SEEN SALVATION:
LIGHT FOR THE GENTILES, GLORY FOR ISRAEL.**

---

29 Lord, let your servant
 now die in peace,
  for you kept your promise.

30 With my own eyes
  I see the salvation
31 you prepared for all peoples:

32 a light of revelation for the Gentiles
  and glory to your people Israel. □

EPHESIANS

CHAPTER 1:3–10

GOD CHOSE US IN CHRIST FOR HOLINESS,
PURCHASING US WITH ABUNDANT LOVE.

---

3 Bless God, the Father of our Lord Jesus Christ,
who blessed us from heaven through Christ
with every blessing of the spirit.

4 Before laying the world's foundation,
God chose us in Christ
to live a pure and holy life.

5 God determined out of love
to adopt us through Jesus Christ
6 for the praise and glory of that grace
granted us in the Beloved.

7 By Christ's blood we were redeemed,
our sins forgiven
8 through extravagant love.

With perfect wisdom and insight
9 God freely displayed the mystery
of what was always intended:
10 a plan for the fullness of time
to unite the entire universe through Christ. □

PHILIPPIANS

CHAPTER 2:6–11

EMPTIED, HUMBLED, OBEDIENT TO THE DEATH,
JESUS EMBRACED THE CROSS:
JESUS CHRIST IS LORD!

---

6 Though in the form of God,
  Jesus did not claim
  equality with God
7 but emptied himself,
  taking the form of a slave,
  human like one of us.

8 Flesh and blood,
  he humbled himself,
  obeying to the death,
  death on a cross.

9 For this very reason
  God lifted him high
  and gave him the name
  above all names.

10 So at the name of Jesus
   every knee will bend
   in heaven, on earth,
   and in the world below,
11 and every tongue exclaim
   to the glory of God the Father,
   "Jesus Christ is Lord."   □

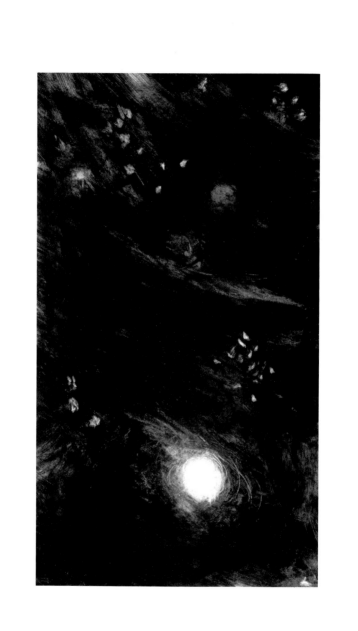

COLOSSIANS

CHAPTER 1:12—20

FIRSTBORN IN ALL CREATION,
FIRSTBORN FROM THE DEAD,
CHRIST OUR PEACE.

12 Give thanks to the Father,
who made us fit
for the holy community of light
13 and rescued us from darkness,
bringing us into the realm
of his beloved Son
14 who redeemed us,
forgiving our sins.

15 Christ is an image
of the God we cannot see.
Christ is firstborn in all creation.

16 Through Christ the universe was made,
things seen and unseen,
thrones, authorities, forces, powers.
Everything was created
through Christ and for Christ.

17 Before anything came to be, Christ was,
and the universe is held together by Christ.

18 Christ is also head of the body, the church,
   its beginning as firstborn from the dead
   to become in all things first.

19 For by God's good pleasure
   Christ encompasses
   the full measure of power,
20 reconciling creation with its source
   and making peace by the blood of the cross.   □

1 TIMOTHY

BASED ON CHAPTER 3:16

PROCLAIM THE MYSTERY OF OUR FAITH!

Astounding mystery
at the heart of our faith:

One who appeared in human flesh, alleluia!
was attested by the Spirit, alleluia!
seen by angels, alleluia!
proclaimed to Gentiles, alleluia!
believed in by the world, alleluia!
taken up in glory, alleluia! ☐

1 PETER

CHAPTER 2:21–24

————————

IN CHRIST, OUR SINS WERE CRUCIFIED.
THROUGH CHRIST, OUR INJURIES WERE HEALED.

———

21 Christ suffered for us
leaving us an example,
that we might walk
in his footsteps.

22 He did nothing wrong;
no false word
ever passed his lips.

23 When they cursed him
he returned no curse.
Tortured, he made no threats
but trusted in the perfect judge.

24 He carried our sins
in his body
to the cross,
that we might die to sin
and live for justice.
When he was wounded,
we were healed.   □

REVELATION

CHAPTERS 4:11; 5:9–10, 12

**BY THE BLOOD OF THE LAMB,
MANY PEOPLES ARE PURCHASED FOR GOD.**

---

11 Worthy are you, Lord God,
   to receive glory, honor and power,
   for you are creator and source of all.

5:9 Worthy are you, O Christ,
   to take the scroll and break the seals,
   for you were slain
   and your blood purchased for God
   every tribe, language, people and nation.

10 You made them royal priests
   to serve our God,
   and they will rule on earth.

12 Worthy is the slaughtered Lamb,
   worthy of power and wealth,
   wisdom and strength,
   honor and glory and praise. □

REVELATION

**THE BATTLE IS WON,
THE ADVERSARY CRINGES IN EXILE
AND CHRIST HOLDS THE POWER.**

---

17 We thank you, Lord,
God and ruler of all,
who are and who were.
You have claimed your power
and begun to reign.

18 When the nations raged
your anger stirred.
Then was the moment
to judge the dead,
to reward your servants, the prophets,
to honor your holy ones
who honored your name,
small and great alike.

12:10b Now is salvation,
the power and reign of God;
the Christ holds command.
For the one who accused the saints
day and night before God
has now been driven out.

11 They won the battle
by the blood of the Lamb
and by the power of their witness
despite the threat of death.
12a Citizens of heaven, rejoice. □

REVELATION

CHAPTERS 15:3—4

BEFORE YOU, O GOD, ALL PEOPLE BOW:
FILLED WITH WONDER, FILLED WITH PRAISE.

3 All you do stirs wonder,
Lord, mighty God.
Your ways are right and true,
ruler of all nations.

4 Who would not be moved
to glorify your name?
For you alone are holy.

All nations will gather,
bowing low to you,
for your saving works
are plainly seen.   □

REVELATION

BASED ON CHAPTER 19:1—7

**GATHER FOR THE FEAST,
THE BELOVED IS HERE. ALLELUIA.**

Alleluia!
Salvation, glory and power to God!
Alleluia, Alleluia!
Right and sure the judgments of God!
Alleluia, Alleluia!

Alleluia!
Praise our God, you faithful servants!
Alleluia, Alleluia!
In awe praise God, you small and great!
Alleluia, Alleluia!

Alleluia!
The Lord God almighty rules!
Alleluia, Alleluia!
Be glad, rejoice, give glory to God!
Alleluia, Alleluia!

Alleluia!
The wedding feast of the Lamb begins.
Alleluia, Alleluia!
The bride is radiant, clothed in glory.
Alleluia, Alleluia!   □

THE CANTICLES OF THE BIBLE

Irene Nowell, OSB

The canticles of both Testaments are poetic prayers embedded within the narrative of the historical books and gospels and within the prose of the letters. These little gems of prayer are also found within the poetry of the prophets' preaching and the sages' wisdom. They appear as resounding hymns in the midst of apocalyptic visions.

The canticles function like a bridge between telling our story and turning to God in prayer. In form and style they resemble the psalms, but they differ from the psalms in their setting. The psalms are separate compositions, only sometimes tied to a context by a brief title. But the canticles are intertwined with their context. These prayers are set in the mouths of specific people in specific situations. They both interrupt the flow of the story and add to its meaning. They are bridges over the gap between life and prayer.

CRIES OF DISTRESS

Crying out to God is a natural response of faithful people when they are confronted by pain and anguish. In the eighth century BCE, the people of Israel faced political insecurity. The Assyrians, a major power, threatened to swallow up their little kingdom. The prophet Hosea warned the people that their suffering was a result of turning away from God, so the people decided to return (Hosea 6:1–6). Their repentance is insincere, however, like "a morning mist, a dew that vanishes early." God reminds them:

> *I take delight*
> *not in sacrifices,*
> *but in loyal love;*
> *not in holocausts,*
> *but in the knowledge of God.*

At the end of the same century, the southern kingdom, Judah, is also threatened by Assyria. The people plead, "Show mercy,

Lord, we look to you" (Isaiah 33:2). The king himself becomes ill, and the prophet Isaiah warns him that he is close to death. King Hezekiah pleads with God for his life (Isaiah 38:10 – 14, 17 – 20). God hears him, and the king regains his health.

At the end of the seventh century BCE, God's people are again threatened by a foreign power, Babylon. The prophet Jeremiah groans in anguish as he sees the destruction of his people (Jeremiah 14:17 – 21). He too pleads with God: "For the sake of your name, do not abandon us" (Jeremiah 14:21; cf. Daniel 3:34). But it is too late. Judah falls to Nebuchadnezzar and the Babylonian army in 587 BCE. Even in the face of this disaster, however, the people cling to God. The poet of Lamentations begs:

> *Why have you forgotten us,*
> *left us alone so long?*
> *Bring us back to you, Lord;*
> *we will gladly come.*
> *Give us good days*
> *like those of old. (Lamentations 5:20 – 21;*
>   *cf. Sirach 36:1 – 7)*

GOD'S PROMISES

The cry to God is not in vain. God meets us on the bridge. The lament of the people of Judah during the Assyrian threat is followed by an oracle of reassurance from God (Isaiah 33:13 – 16). God will save the people, but they must remain faithful. "Terror grips the wicked." It is "only the honest" who "can face the fiery judgment."

More than a century later, God again comes to save the people (Isaiah 63:1 – 5), "striding along with great power" to "bring news of . . . victory." When the enemy is no more, God turns to the suffering people with promise. The prophet Ezekiel carries that promise to the exiles in sixth-century Babylon (Ezekiel 36:24 – 28). God will bathe this defeated and disheartened people in fresh water, give them new hearts, breathe new spirit into them. In God's new creation, they will again breathe with the breath of

God and live in the land God gives them. The covenant promise will be renewed:

> *You will be my people*
> *and I will be your God.*

SONGS OF THANKSGIVING

The response to God's salvation is thanksgiving. In all circumstances, whether the deliverance from distress is personal or communal, God's people sing their gratitude.

Hannah, a barren wife, poured out her troubles to God before the ark of the covenant. God remembered Hannah and she gave birth to a son, Samuel, the future judge-prophet of Israel. Hannah's song of thanksgiving (1 Samuel 2:1 – 10) moves from gratitude for her own son to praise for God's universal power. Hannah regards her own experience as evidence that God's special care is for the poor and lowly:

> *The weapons of the strong are broken,*
> *the defenseless gain strength.*
> *The overfed now toil to eat,*
> *while the hungry have their fill.*
> *The childless bear many children,*
> *but the fertile learn they are sterile.*

Some songs of thanksgiving are songs of the entire people. When God delivers the thirteenth-century Israelites from slavery in Egypt by leading them through the sea, Miriam leads them in the song "The Lord is my strength, the Lord who saves me" (Exodus 15:2). Isaiah puts the song in the mouths of the eighth-century people freed from fear of the Assyrians (Isaiah 12:1 – 6). Jeremiah foresees a new song for the sixth-century people released from the Babylonian exile:

> *God gathers the scattered flock,*
> *guides Israel like a shepherd. (Jeremiah 31:10)*

In the Book of Isaiah there are songs of thanksgiving for a new king (probably Hezekiah) and songs of thanksgiving for the restoration of Jerusalem after the exile. The new king brings light to "the people who walk in darkness" (Isaiah 9:1 – 6). Restored Jerusalem sings out "like a groom wearing a garland or a bride arrayed in jewels" (Isaiah 61:10).

The song of thanksgiving is a bold cry of faith even as disaster threatens. In the apocalyptic vision of the Book of Revelation, thanksgiving appears between the woes. In the midst of chaos, voices from heaven sing:

> We thank you, Lord,
> God and ruler of all,
> who are and who were.
> You have claimed your power
> and begun to reign. (Revelation 11:17)

The battle that now rages has already been won. God's people have the courage to sing their thanksgiving even when they are still suffering persecution. Their song is testimony to their unshakable confidence that God will deliver them. Deliverance is such a sure thing that it is safe to give thanks now for God's future gifts.

PRAYERS OF TRUST

Prayers of trust flow from longer reflections than songs of thanksgiving. The bridge has been crossed many times: God has saved, not only once, but again and again. Repeated deliverance leads to a gradual awareness of the immensity of God's love and fidelity. God will never fail us.

The Book of Isaiah is filled with prayers of trust. The sixth-century prophet of chapters 40 – 55 encourages the people to hope for the end of the Babylonian exile. God is the one who "can scoop up the oceans or span the heavens with one hand" (Isaiah 40:12). This all-powerful God tends the flock of Israel like a gentle shepherd. God, who created the heavens and formed the earth, says, "I am the Lord. There is no other" (Isaiah 45:18). God will bring the people home, "will cut a mountain road, build a level highway" for them (Isaiah 49:11).

Hope for God's victory over Babylon leads to visions of life for the people after God's final victory over all the evils that afflict humankind (Isaiah 26:1 – 4, 7 – 9, 12). Their "city is strong, its ramparts and walls are God's saving work." The faithful are guarded in peace; God makes their road "level, smooth, and straight." God promises to reward the people with "a lasting covenant" (Isaiah 61:8):

> *All who see them will say*
> *they are blest by the Lord (Isaiah 61:9).*

The New Testament vision of the end of time leads also to a prayer of trust:

> *All you do stirs wonder,*
> *Lord, mighty God.*
> *Your ways are right and true,*
> *ruler of all nations. (Revelation 15:3)*

This song occurs too in the midst of trouble. The prayer of trust soars over the vision of the seven angels carrying the seven plagues. Still the visionary can proclaim: "Your saving works are plainly seen" (Revelation 15:4).

WISDOM MEDITATIONS

Sometimes wise people stand on the bridge to ponder the ways of God and the experiences of life. The juxtaposition of the two leads to insight. Topics range across the breadth of human life. What about wealth?

> *Happy are the rich*
> *who still have their integrity,*
> *who are not corrupted by money. (Sirach 31:8)*

What happens to those who die?

> *In our mortal view,*
> *they were punished,*
> *but they gained what they hoped for:*
> *never ending life. (Wisdom 3:4)*

In what should we trust?

> *Put no trust in this lie:*
> *The temple of the Lord!*

The temple of the Lord!
The temple will save me! (Jeremiah 7:4)

They are blest who trust in God,
who trust in the Lord alone.
They are like trees near a stream
stretching their roots to the water. (Jeremiah 17:7)

One such wisdom meditation is set on the lips of Moses as a farewell speech at the time of his death (Deuteronomy 32:1 – 12). He ponders the goodness of God and the foolishness of human beings. Yet even human folly cannot defeat God's goodness. Like a mother eagle carrying her young, God carries Israel. "There is no other God."

It is through Wisdom that God saves the people throughout the ages. Wisdom "brought them through the Reed Sea" (Wisdom 10:18). Through Wisdom, God cared for the people in the desert and fed them "food for angels" (Wisdom 16:20). It is Wisdom herself who is this bread of life. She has built her house, prepared the meal, and invited her guests (Proverbs 9:1 – 6, 10 – 12).

The Jerusalem teacher, Ben Sira proclaims:

Happy those who feast on Wisdom
and savor her knowledge.
She will nourish and refresh them:
her bread is insight,
her drink is understanding. (Sirach 14:20; 15:3)

The sages unanimously advise the search for Wisdom (see Sirach 39:13 – 16). The author of the Book of Wisdom gives us a prayer for her.

Send her from heaven,
from your glorious throne
to be my companion,
to teach me your will. (Wisdom 9:10)

A hymn in the Letter to the Colossians presents Christ as Wisdom:

Christ is an image
of the God we cannot see.

> *Everything was created*
> *through Christ and for Christ. (Colossians 1:15 – 16)*

The mystery is this: Christ is Wisdom incarnate, Wisdom in our human flesh (1 Timothy 3:16). His taking on of our human experience is total:

> *Though in the form of God,*
> *Jesus did not claim*
> *equality with God*
> *but emptied himself,*
> *taking the form of a slave,*
> *human like one of us. (Philomon 2:6 – 7)*

Through Christ, Wisdom incarnate, God has been "reconciling creation with its source and making peace by the blood of the cross" (Colossians 1:20). Wisdom incarnate teaches us how to live a fully human life:

> *Christ suffered for us*
> *leaving us an example,*
> *that we might walk in his footsteps. (1 Peter 2:21)*

HYMNS OF PRAISE

The bridge leads finally to praise. God's people give praise in a variety of situations. There are individuals whose lives have been saved by God. Tobit, who has been healed of blindness and whose daughter-in-law has been delivered from a demon, calls out to God's people scattered across the world to join him in praise (Tobit 13:1 – 7). The three young men thrown into the fiery furnace by the soldiers of King Nebuchadnezzar praise God for delivering them from the flames (Daniel 3:52 – 57). Their hymn becomes a call to all creation to join in the praise: stars, angels, fire, fish, birds, beasts (Daniel 3:56 – 88).

Individual prayers, however, are never far from the awareness of the whole community. Both Tobit and the three young men stand as symbols for the entire people. Judith sings a hymn of praise to God, who strengthened her hand so that she might assassinate Holofernes and save her people from destruction (Judith 16:2 – 3, 13 – 15). A prophet in the Book of Isaiah describes God delivering the exiles from Babylon (Isaiah 42:10 – 16):

> *The Lord strides like a hero*
> *who rouses fury*
> *with a great battle cry*
> *and charges against the enemy.*

Babylon becomes the universal symbol for the great enemy in a New Testament victory hymn. After the destruction of Babylon, a great multitude in heaven sings in praise of God: "Salvation, glory and power to God!" (Revelation 19:1)

Some hymns praise Jerusalem, God's city, and the temple within it. When the people have brought their generous offerings for the building of the temple, David praises God for making these gifts possible (1 Chronicles 29:10 – 13). Tobit, exiled in Nineveh, sees his healing as a sign of the restoration of Jerusalem (Tobit 13:8 – 11, 13 – 15). There is a hymn to the new Jerusalem at the beginning and the end of the Book of Isaiah (Isaiah 2:2 – 5; 66:10 – 14).

The New Testament canticles declare that it is in and through Christ that all peoples will be delivered from their enemies and united as one (Revelation 4:11; 5:9 – 10, 12). This is the mystery of God's great plan for us from the beginning of time:

> *With perfect wisdom and insight*
> *God freely displayed the mystery*
> *of what was always intended:*
> *a plan for the fullness of time*
> *to unite the entire universe through Christ.*
> *(Ephesians 1:8 – 10)*

THE DAILY CANTICLES

There remain three privileged canticles from the Gospel of Luke. These three songs of thanksgiving are sung daily in the Liturgy of the Hours: the canticle of Zechariah at morning prayer (Luke 1:69 – 75), the canticle of Mary at evening prayer (Luke 1:46 – 55), and the canticle of Simeon at compline (Luke 2:29 – 32). With these three canticles the praying church celebrates each day this mystery: God taking on our human flesh that we might share the life of God.

Mary's canticle is set within the story of her visit to her cousin Elizabeth. The two pregnant women greet each other; John leaps in Elizabeth's womb in recognition of Jesus in the womb of Mary. Elizabeth proclaims Mary blessed, and Mary sings this song of ecstatic praise. Her song, based on the song of Hannah (1 Samuel 2:1 – 10), celebrates God's turning the world topsy-turvy. The rich are hungry, the poor are filled. The powerful are thrown down, the insignificant are given power. The greatest reversal of all is the reason for her song: The all-mighty God takes on the lowliness of human existence. Every evening, as we end our day with all-too-human flaws and griefs, we sing of the amazing humility of God, who has shared this life with us.

Zechariah was struck dumb at the angel's announcement that he and Elizabeth would have a son. When the baby is born, Zechariah's tongue is loosed and he breaks forth in praise. His song is fitting for the celebration of the boy's circumcision, for he recalls God's faithfulness to the covenant throughout the ages. He exclaims in wonder at the role this child will play in God's ongoing plan: "You will come to prepare a pathway for the Lord." Every morning, as we enter a new day, we recall with Zechariah God's untiring faithfulness and mercy. We do not face the day alone. God has come to share it with us.

Luke tells also of how Mary and Joseph took the child to the temple to offer the customary sacrifices for the redemption of the firstborn and the purification of the mother. In the temple they meet two faithful elderly people, Simeon and Anna, who recognize Jesus as the messiah. Simeon sings his gratitude to God: "Let your servant now die in peace, for you kept your promise." This traditional night prayer is a trusting surrender of our lives to our faithful God. Sleep is a rehearsal for death. We relinquish control to God. With Simeon we fall gratefully into the hands of God, our God who always keeps promises.

THE CANTICLES OF OUR LIVES

The canticles are a bridge between life experience and prayer. Individuals cry out to God in sickness, in persecution, under siege. The whole people cries out for deliverance from enemies.

We raise our voices and speak for all in need. God promises salvation and keeps the promise. The response from the covenant people is thanksgiving and growing trust in this faithful God. The mystery of God's presence and action among us is food for meditation and finally breaks out in wondering praise. The mystery culminates in Jesus, who came to teach us the new song of life with God. Alleluia!

AFTERWORD

The idea for this liturgical psalter project was initiated in 1964 when the International Commission on English in the Liturgy (ICEL) received its mandate approved by English-speaking conferences of bishops. Among the principal charges given to ICEL in that mandate was the provision of biblical texts used in the liturgy. ICEL's first response to this aspect of its mandate was the issuance in 1967 of "English for the Mass: Part II," which contained a translation of four psalms (Psalms 25, 34, 85 and 130) and guidelines for the preparation of a liturgical psalter.

In "English for the Mass: Part II" it was explained that ICEL would undertake this project because of the special need for a text for singing. The book also listed principles that would guide the work as it developed in later years:

(1) The best existing versions both critical and literary should be consulted.
(2) Greater freedom should be allowed in translating psalms than most books of the Bible because they are poetry and must be such in English and because they are meant for the frequent and inspiring use of the people, choirs, and cantors in the liturgy.
(3) Rhythm suited to the English language should be used in the translation.

The need to provide countless vernacular texts of the various rites in a short period of time delayed the beginning of this project for another decade. Other modern English Bible translations were readily available; and the episcopal conferences of English-speaking countries authorized the psalter of one or more of these for liturgical use in their regions. The Book of Psalms from *The Jerusalem Bible, The New American Bible, The Revised Standard Version,* and also the Grail translation of the psalms provided the texts which have been used in the liturgy of the hours and for the responsorial psalm in the liturgy of the word for the past 25 or 30 years. In 1978 ICEL's Advisory Committee (the general steering committee for all ICEL projects) received authorization from the Episcopal Board (ICEL's chief governing body made up of a bishop-representative from the 11 English-speaking member conferences of bishops) to establish a sub-committee on the liturgical psalter. Initially this subcommittee was asked to produce a statement of purposes and procedures and to provide a translation of ten psalms, representative of the various genres of psalms contained in the Book of Psalms. The members of the subcommittee included specialists in Hebrew language and poetry, liturgical history and theology, music, English poetry, and literary and language theory. Together they wrote an initial 15-page "Brief," and then undertook the translation of the first group of ten psalms. Literal and base translations were produced by the Hebraists and, in dialogue with the poets, liturgists, literary critics and musicians of the team, the texts were continually refined. In late 1981 a consultation booklet was printed which included the translation of ten psalms, their musical settings, liturgical comments on their use, explanatory textual notes and a questionnaire. This was sent to a wide variety of liturgical communities and professionals for comment and evaluation after trial use during the Easter season of 1982.

During this first limited consultation, the translation team continued its work on another set of texts, taking into account responses to the questionnaire as they became available. By Easter 1984 a larger set of 22 psalms (those most often used in the liturgy) were sent out for more extensive consultation to two thousand worship commissions, parishes, religious communities and schools in the English-speaking world. On the basis of the positive responses received in these two consultations the Episcopal Board in 1986 asked for immediate wider circulation of the psalms already completed. In 1987, 23 psalms were published, under the title *Psalms for All Seasons: From the ICEL Liturgical Psalter Project,* by the Pastoral Press in Washington D.C. The Episcopal Board at that time also authorized the completion of the full project.

To facilitate the translation of the remaining psalms and canticles according to the principles outlined in the Brief, four working groups were organized (in London, New York, Chicago, and

Washington D.C.). Each group was composed of five members who possessed the various specialties necessary for the scope of the project. When a working group judged that the texts it was assigned were in presentable form, they were circulated to colleagues in each of the three other working groups for their review and written comments. This material was sent to a five-person Editorial Committee constituted from among the members of the working groups. The committee would review the comments and make any changes in the texts deemed necessary. The Editorial Committee would then circulate these next-to-final draft texts to the ICEL Advisory Committee for its review, comments, and approval. The Editorial Committee would then arrive at a final draft text on the basis of these comments.

The aims of those who have worked on this project were to create a translation (1) that would faithfully render into English the best critical Hebrew and Greek texts available; (2) that would be guided by the liturgical use of the psalms and canticles, and be fitting for musical setting; (3) that would be received by the reader or auditor as idiomatic English in contemporary poetic style; and (4) that would be sensitive to evolving gender usage in English, for example, as described in the "Criteria for the Evaluation of Inclusive Language Translations of Scriptural Texts Proposed for Liturgical Use" of the National Conference of Catholic Bishops of the United States.

I. FAITHFUL RENDERING

To assure the accuracy and integrity of the new translation, the translators have worked at all stages of the process from the Masoretic text (Biblia Hebraica Stuttgartensia). In those frequent cases where the Masoretic text is not certain or clear in meaning, significant help was provided by the witness of ancient translations (for example, the Septuagint and Vulgate), and by the expanded vocabulary and stylistic usages found in ancient nonbiblical documents of the Semitic language area.

Because this translation is intended for contemporary liturgical use, it follows the principles of dynamic equivalence, rather than formal equivalence. As any serious effort at translation, it seeks: to render accurately the meaning of the original, to convey the spirit and nuances of the original, to make complete sense in idiomatic English and achieve a certain literary quality, and, as far as possible, to produce the same effect in modern readers as the original Hebrew produced in its audience. The key to a dynamic equivalence translation, however, is a more acute awareness that a modern receptor language expresses the thought, nuances, and presuppositions of its society in modes that are often different from those of ancient societies. Thus, while a formally equivalent translation seeks to render closely the distinctive structural and semantic characteristics of the source language (for example, grammatical and rhetorical constructions, word order, tense, number and gender markers, literal translation of idioms not found in the receptor language), a dynamically equivalent translation seeks parallel structural, semantic and idiomatic units that are native to the receptor language. Indeed, to communicate as closely as possible the very content of the psalm or canticle to an English-speaking audience, ancient rhetorical structures and grammatical forms must be adapted to English modes of expression.

Particular mention must be made of a central characteristic of the Hebrew text of the psalms that does not have a direct parallel in English: namely, the use of the Tetragrammaton (YHWH) as the unvoiced Hebrew name for God. Out of respect for the traditional Jewish reverence for this name, it is not used in this translation. Instead, following current scholarly understanding of the divine name(s), "God" and "Lord" are used somewhat interchangeably to translate "YHWH", "adonay", and "elohim". In the Hebrew Scriptures "God" and "Lord" are often used as parallel terms (Exodus 15:17; Deuteronomy 7:9; 2 Kings 19:4; Isaiah 3:17; Psalms 7:9–10; 35:22; 71:5). Different stages of development of the Scriptures also show different practices in the use of the divine name, as does the practice of the Greek translators of the Septuagint who offered varied renderings. For example, Hebrew "YHWH" is translated as "theos" in Septuagint Genesis 4:16; 6:7, and in Psalm 70 (71):1; while Hebrew "elohim" is translated as "kurios" in Septuagint Genesis 21:2, 6; 48:15; and Psalm 76 (77):2.

The choice of "Lord" and "God" in this translation is influenced by this tradition, as well as by considerations central to this project: the principles of a dynamically equivalent translation, of modern English style noted for its compression of language, and of poetry with its attention to poetic rhythm, repetition and/or variation.

II. A LITURGICAL TRANSLATION
FOR MUSICAL ACCOMPANIMENT

This translation takes into account the original liturgical contexts of these works (e.g. lament, thanksgiving, wisdom, enthronement psalms), as well as their traditional use in Christian worship.

Because these texts are essentially liturgical works, their translation presumes musical performance as the norm, though they would also be suitable for choral recitation and private devotion. Special care is given to the sounds of words, their sequence and rhythm, as well as to their sense, not only for poetic purposes but also that they might be attractive to composers and musicians.

Decisions as to the division of strophes, use of refrains, syllabic count and distribution of stresses within a line were made according to the nature of the text under consideration, its use in the liturgy, and the poetic judgment of the translating group. A certain regularity of stress pattern was sought as desirable but was not slavishly applied. More than two unstressed syllables between stressed syllables were avoided wherever possible, as were lame cadences. Stressed final syllables were preferred at endline, and diphthongs were avoided. Care was also taken to facilitate singing by rejecting words and word sequences with consonantal clusters difficult to articulate.

III. TRANSLATION INTO CONTEMPORARY
ENGLISH POETIC STYLE

Keeping to the principle of dynamic equivalence, this translation seeks to render the psalms and canticles in a style that is idiomatically English and in a contemporary poetic form marked by heightened imagery and concision. The translators sought a balance between a vernacular language that would be immediately communicative and a poetic liturgical language that would draw people out of their familiar worlds and elucidate their ordinary experience.

Toward this end efforts are made in this translation to bring to the surface metaphors that are submerged in the original language and in other translations. The attempt is made to render these metaphors with the same immediacy and concreteness they possessed in the original. The vocabulary exhibits a strong preference for monosyllables and Anglo-Saxon root words, rather than words of Latinate origin. The liveliness of the Hebrew texts is conveyed through the use of a wider variety of striking concrete verbs than is found in other translations. These often serve as the vehicle for the metaphors and imagery, and their energy is preserved by being frequently in the present tense.

A well-known structural component of Hebrew poetry is the use of parallelism in its various forms: synonymous, antithetical or synthetic (in which there is no strict parallel as such, but rather a close connection of logic or consequence or addition). Most psalms employ the last type and thus cannot be said to employ simply two matching expressions that reiterate the same thought. Translators thus need to recognize several possible levels of meaning in Hebrew couplets and not think that a merely mechanical reproduction of paired lines always represents an adequate rendering of the text. Furthermore, though the occasional use of parallelism and other rhetorical figures are certainly not foreign to modern poetry, a consistent use of such figures would strike a contemporary reader with the stateliness, but also the remoteness and stasis of the Augustan verse of the eighteenth century.

To achieve a more contemporary poetic style, this translation employs a number of strategies to deal with parallelisms: first, word order is sometimes changed, and the second subject is absorbed into the first or replaced by a pronoun. Thus, the strictly parallel form A:B:C::A:B:C might appear as A:B:C::B:C or A:B:C::(a):B:C, as in Psalm 72:9:

> Literal Hebrew:
> *Before him shall bow down the siyyim (meaning unclear)*
> *And his enemies the dust will lick.*

> ICEL translation:
> *Enemies will cower before him,*
> *they will lick the dust.*

Second, enjambment is used to run the thought of two parallel lines into a continuous sentence, as in Psalm 47:6:

> Literal Hebrew:
> *God goes up to shouts of praise;*
> *the Lord to the sound of the trumpet.*

> ICEL translation:
> *God ascends the mountain*
> *to cheers and trumpet blasts.*
>
> (Note that "mountain" is added here for the sake of clarity for a modern audience who might otherwise think God is ascending to the heavens rather than to the temple on Mount Zion.)

Through all these various means, this translation hopes to render the psalms and canticles in a contemporary English poetic and liturgical style that is in the spirit of the direction given by the Holy See's 1969 Instruction on the Translation of Liturgical Texts:

> *The prayer of the church is always the prayer of some actual community, assembled here and now. It is not sufficient that a formula handed down from some other time or region be translated verbatim, even if accurately, for liturgical use. The formula translated must become the genuine prayer of the congregation and in it each of its members should be able to find and express himself or herself (no. 20).*

IV. INCLUSIVE LANGUAGE

One of the most notable characteristics of contemporary English-speaking communities is a growing sensitivity to gender-exclusive language. The psalms, in particular, reflect the prayer of the temple liturgy that was voiced by an all-male assembly; their expression consequently is influenced by the experience, imaginative vision and language of their originating congregation. Even so, this cultic perspective conceals the memory recorded elsewhere in the Old Testament of the women of Israel as faithful devotees, songwriters, and leaders of song for the covenant community: e.g., Miriam (Exodus 15:20–21), Hannah (1 Samuel 2:1–10), and Judith (Judith 16:1–17). Surely a liturgical psalter that is to serve the living faith of a covenant community manifestly composed of men and women ought neither impede nor distort the good news of God's all-inclusive embrace by using discriminatory language. In accord with the principles and linguistic strategies of the "Criteria for the Evaluation of Inclusive Language Translations of Scriptural Texts Proposed for Liturgical Use" (hereafter, CEILT) this translation attempts to "facilitate the full, conscious and active participation of all members of the church, women and men, in worship" (CEILT, no. 13).

Specifically, the generic "he" of the psalms and canticles is translated variously according to the organizing metaphors and internal shifts of person, number and voice manifested in a particular text. Thus in context it may be rendered "I" or "we," "you" or "they" (see CEILT, no. 23).

Furthermore, words no longer understood as inclusive terms, such as "man" or "men," "sons," "brothers" or "brethren," and "forefathers," are avoided (CEILT, nos. 18–19), except where demanded by a particular context. Thus, psalms and canticles that refer to historic males, females and institutions continue to do so in this translation, as in the specific reference to the king in Psalm 72, and to the king, queen, and inheritance customs of Psalm 45:

> *Your sons will inherit*
> *the throne your fathers held. (v. 17)*

Likewise, when the feminine personification of Zion (and the accompanying implicit feminization of the chosen people relative to a divine masculine) is integral to the imagery and meaning of the psalm, this translation honors the operative convention. Thus, Psalm 87:5 is rendered, "Zion mothered each and every one"; without this metaphor, there is no psalm.

This translation also addresses the problem of naming God and has followed the direction of the CEILT, no. 26:

> Great care should be taken in translations of the names
> of God and in the use of pronouns referring to God.
> While it would be inappropriate to attribute
> gender to God as such, the revealed word of God
> consistently uses a masculine reference for God. It may
> sometimes be useful, however, to repeat the name of
> God, as used earlier in the text, rather than to use the
> masculine pronoun in every case. But care must
> be taken that the repetition not become tiresome.

In order to deal with direct references to God's name, several strategies have been developed and employed in this translation: (1) The approach to the rendering of the Tetragrammaton YHWH has been discussed above in Section I. (2) Some of the more pervasive and important titles of God, such as "Lord," "King," "Shepherd," are usually retained because they have significant historical and theological resonances that would otherwise be lost. (3) Wherever possible, masculine pronouns are not used to refer to God. Instead: (a) the name itself might be repeated or a synonym provided ("God" or "the Lord"); (b) judging from internal shifts of grammatical person manifested in a particular text, the third person ("he") might be absorbed into a continuous second-person ("you") form throughout the entire psalm or canticle (CEILT, no. 23); (c) or, most commonly, the linguistic structure is arranged in idiomatic English such that the need for a pronominal expression never arises. (4) Finally, this translation seeks to highlight vividly the metaphors of the original texts that reveal God as recognizably personal: a God who acts and whose self is revealed by action. Thus, the verbs attributed to God in this translation, as in the source texts, are strikingly anthropomorphic: a playful God "rides the clouds" (Psalm 68:5); a providential God "blocks the plans of nations" (Psalm 33:10), but "steadies the faithful" (Psalm 37:23); an angry God seethes (Psalm 78:21), and bellows (Psalm 18:16), while a compassionate God "keeps a loving eye" on the faithful (Psalm 33:18), "enfolds" them "with tender care" (Psalm 103:4), and "stands by victims" (Psalm 109:31). Yet the mystery of God's existence remains: a personal existence that embraces and yet transcends gendered human existence (see CEILT, no. 28). Thus, in this rendering as in the original, God is figured "like a king" (Psalm 95:3), "a warrior" (Psalm 78:65), but also "a nesting bird" (Psalm 91:4); God "fathers" (Deuteronomy 32:6, Tobit 13:4), but can love "like a mother" (Psalm 106:46).

CONCLUSION

The aim of this lively poetry crafted especially for the contemporary liturgical assembly is to make the psalter sing the church into a new recognition of the mystery of God still at work in daily life. If the translations have any value, and if composers set them imaginatively for the communities they serve, they will lead to a more vital manifestation of that eternal mystery.

THE DESIGN

This volume complements *The Psalter*. As designer, my responsibility was to maintain the integrity of Kerry Perlmutter's original work while adapting it to the new content. *The Canticles* is thus one of this pair of books, both enduring in their visual and tactile qualities.

The design seeks symmetry and balance, each page set to suggest a visual center and to create a graceful presentation of the canticles. The text was typeset patiently and precisely by Karen Mitchell in Minion, a contemporary face inspired by classic old style faces, designed in 1992 by Robert Slimbach. As much attention has been given to the quality of the materials as to the crafts of type and design. The pages of the book were printed by Thiessen Printing Corp. of Chicago on 70 pound Somerset Matte Text. The casebound editions were bound at Zonne Bookbinders, Inc., of Chicago.

Anna Manhart

THE ART

Because this volume of canticles is a companion to *The Psalter*, I thought it important to make a connection visually. The artwork serves as a continuum.

The art on these pages are reproductions of monotypes. Black etching ink is spread across a smooth zinc plate, then wiped away using a brush, cloth and palette-knife to create or to uncover an image. Only one original print is the result of this process, and the plate is again covered with ink for the making of the next image.

The canticles in this volume incorporate such similar images, sounds, moods and movements to the psalms that I again found myself influenced by the themes of landscape and nature, shelter and phenomena, energy and mystery. As well, the people whose voices have carried these words down through the ages served as both inspiration and subject for the art. The scale of the images runs from a close, intimate range to one that is vast and sweeping. As an artist, my fervent hope is to create a setting that the participant can enter and so find inspiration while reading and singing these beautiful prayers. In both *The Psalter* and *The Canticles* the words hold the priority; the art complements as respite while we pray.

Linda Ekstrom